Robyn Trostle

Illustrator Mary Carrell

XULON ELITE

Xulon Press Elite
2301 Lucien Way #415
Maitland, FL 32751
407.339.4217
www.xulonpress.com

© 2022 by Robyn Trostle

All rights reserved solely by the author. The author guarantees all contents are original and do not infringe upon the legal rights of any other person or work. No part of this book may be reproduced in any form without the permission of the author.

Due to the changing nature of the Internet, if there are any web addresses, links, or URLs included in this manuscript, these may have been altered and may no longer be accessible. The views and opinions shared in this book belong solely to the author and do not necessarily reflect those of the publisher. The publisher therefore disclaims responsibility for the views or opinions expressed within the work.

Unless otherwise indicated, Scripture quotations taken from the New King James Version (NKJV). Copyright © 1982 by Thomas Nelson, Inc. Used by permission. All rights reserved.

Paperback ISBN-13: 978-1-6628-4705-9
Hard Cover ISBN-13: 978-1-6628-5198-8
Ebook ISBN-13: 978-1-6628-4706-6

We can read a passage of scripture and learn something new each time we read it. That is certainly what happened when I read Psalm 139 a few years ago. It spoke to me very deeply and it was as if I was reading it for the first time, which is what started me on the journey of writing this book. A person can be loved by others without really feeling love for themselves. I longed for love and acceptance, and I believed I could gain these through my accomplishments. As I struggled with insecurities, there were times I felt unworthy, unloved, and had a terrible self-image. Nothing was ever good enough in my eyes. I was a child of God, but the devil was "devouring" me daily and stealing my joy (I Peter 5:8-10). But there is healing in God's Word, and that is exactly what I found in Psalm 139. It helped me understand I am very special to God and that He loves me just as I am. My prayer is that anyone who reads this book would understand His amazing love for all of us and how very special we are to Him. Everyone is precious to God!

When I first began writing this book it was just about Psalm 139, a passage which describes how deeply God loves and cares about us. Through further reading and studying through Genesis 1 & 2 and the Psalms, it has grown to include the story of creation in the order as it occurred in Genesis, and as it is reflected in the Psalms.

Since the beginning of time, God has revealed Himself to us through creation. We can simply look at the beauty of nature and know He exists because of the world He has created around us. This is how it all began.

God was there even before the mountains or the
earth were made. He was ALWAYS there.

Then, the Lord spoke and by His command the heavens, the earth, the seas, and everything in them were created. So whenever you enjoy the beauty of a crystal blue sky, feel the lush green grass between your toes, or experience the crashing of the waves in the ocean; remember that God simply breathed a word and they came into existence.

Next, He made the great lights—the sun and the moon.
Day and night are His because He made them.

Then, He stretched out the heavens like a curtain.
In the heavens, He rides on the clouds as if they are
His chariot, and He walks on the wings of the wind.

He made the earth's foundation so it would never be moved.
The waters were high above the mountains and at His word,
the waters fled. The mountains and the earth were uncovered,
and the waters went to the places He told them to go.

When God looks at the earth it trembles.
When He touches the mountains, they smoke.

He allows the springs to flow into the valleys where He makes the grass and plants grow. When beautiful fields of flowers and trees are swaying back and forth with the wind, it's as if they are joyful with praise and are rejoicing before Him, because He made them.

In the heavens, He placed the moon and the stars.
He created the moon to mark the seasons.
He numbers the stars and calls them by name.

He alone makes the summer and the winter.

He also created the north and the south. Just as the heavens are high above the earth, God's love and mercy are never-ending for those who put their trust in Him. He takes their sin and puts it as far away from them as the east is from the west.

He tells the sun when to go down and it is evening. He makes the darkness and it is night. This is when He allows the earth to come alive with more of His creation—cicadas, crickets and katydids singing their own songs of praise. Then, as the morning dawns there is rejoicing as birds and insects sing to the heavens and declare His glory.

He sent forth His spirit and all the animals were created.

Every beast of the field and forest belong to Him.

Everything is His for He created it all.

Even the cattle on a thousand hills are His.

They live in His creation where He gives water for the wild donkeys to drink. The young lions run after their prey and God gives them their food. He makes the high hills a home for the wild goats and the cliffs are home to the rock badgers.

The deer roam in the fields seeking food and water.
Just as the deer pants for water, so do we
also long for God and His presence.

He knows all the birds of the mountains.
They make their nests and sing in the branches of the trees.

Lastly, He created man to have authority over all His creation. The Lord looks down from heaven and sees everything He created. He looks at all the people He created on the earth. He made each heart individually.

He created you to be very special to Him. He loves you just like you are. There is nothing you could do that would make Him love you more, and you cannot do anything to make Him love you less. God also looks at you deeply and knows everything about you. He knows each and every one of us by name. Wow, the God of the whole universe knows your name! What a wonderful God He is! How Amazing is His love for you!

You are very special to God. He knows how you are feeling all the time. He knows the secrets you keep way down deep in your heart. He knows you even better than you know yourself.

You are very special to God. He knows everything you are doing every minute of the day—whether you are playing, eating, or sleeping. He cares about everything you are doing all the time. There may be times when you are feeling scared and do not want to be in your room alone. When this happens, remember God cares that you are scared, and He does not want you to be afraid. He also wants you to remember that He is always with you.

He always knows what you are thinking every minute of every day. He knows if you have good thoughts or bad thoughts. He will help you not to think about things that are wrong if you will keep your thoughts on Him.

You are very special to God. He knows when you are feeling happy, and He knows when you are feeling sad. When you cry, He places your tears into a bottle. He is always close to those who have a broken heart, even though you may not feel like He is there. He will never leave you! What a wonderful God He is! How amazing is His love for you!

You are very special to God. He knows what you are going to say, even before you say it. May the words and the thoughts of your heart always be pleasing to Him. He knows when you say a kind or unkind word, even before it comes out of your mouth. May you always put a guard over your mouth and watch over what comes across your lips.

You are very special to God. He surrounds you with His love and He is your protector. You can lean on Him in times of trouble. He wraps His arms around you, and under the shadow of His wings you are sheltered and secure. He entrusts you to His angels who watch over you and help lift you up and keep you from harm.

It is hard to understand how much He loves and cares about you. The love of God is beyond your wildest imagination. His love is so deep that it reaches far down into the depths of your soul and pours out over you like a waterfall. It washes over you like waves in the ocean. His loving kindness is better than life. Praise Him with your lips and bless Him while you live. What a wonderful God He is! How amazing is His love for you!

You are very special to God. He is always with you no matter where you are going or what you are doing. No matter how high you go—whether climbing a mountain or even soaring up into space, God is with you, for the heights of the hills belong to Him. No matter how low you go—even into the depths of the Earth, God is with you for in His hand are the deep places of the Earth.

Self-portrait of Mary Carrell, Illustrator

If you are flying on a plane, soaring high above the clouds, God is with you. If you are exploring the deepest, darkest part of the ocean, God is with you, as the sea is His because He made it. There is nowhere you can go that He is not with you—you are never alone. He is always with you, showing you where to go. Even when you are worried or scared, you have no reason to fear for He is with you and He comforts you. Even when there is darkness, and you are afraid, sick, or hurting, He is the shining light in the midst of darkness. He will help you!

God holds you in His hand and gives you His strength and guidance. He makes His footsteps your pathway. Walking in His footsteps will help lead you in the right direction in your life.

He is the God who does wonders, so He made you and hid you in your mother's womb. There you were warm and protected until you were born into the world. Praise Him and thank Him for creating you to be who you are—very special and very unique in your own way.

He could see you when you were very small, when you were still being formed. All the days of your life were written in His book even before you were born. So try to learn more about God and live for Him each day. Learn to make each day count for Him! What a wonderful God He is! How amazing is His love for you!

You are very special to God. It is amazing to think the God of the universe should think about you, and yet He does! He thinks about you all the time! You are His creation and His thoughts toward you are more than ALL the sand in ALL of the oceans—too numerous to count! What a wonderful God He is! How amazing is His love for you!

You are very special to God. No matter where you are, He is always there with you—always. He never leaves you. He looks deeply at your heart and will show you where you need to improve if you will ask Him. Maybe you need to have a better attitude, share more with others, or show someone you really love and care about them.

He will show you what He wants you to do, and where He wants you to go if you will open your heart and follow Him. When you live for Him you will have complete joy. What a wonderful God He is! How amazing is His love for you!

Because of His amazing love and since He is creator of all, you will praise Him from the heavens, and you will praise Him from the earth. You will praise Him from the heights, and you will praise Him from the depths.

The sun, moon, and the stars will praise Him.

Fire, hail, snow, and the clouds will praise Him.
Even the wind will praise Him.

The mountains and trees will praise Him.

The beasts of the field and all the cattle will praise Him.
Even the creeping things and birds will praise Him.

Painting of the author, Robyn Trostle, age 9, and childhood friend

Kings, princes and all the people of the earth will praise Him.

Men and women, young and old will praise Him.

Children will praise Him.

From sunrise to sunset, His name is to be praised.

"Let everything that has breath praise the Lord." – Psalm 150:6

What a wonderful God He is!
How Amazing is His love for you!

CPSIA information can be obtained
at www.ICGtesting.com
Printed in the USA
LVHW072055090622
720907LV00007B/100